CONTENTS

INTRODUCTION	7
DO YOU BELIEVE IN MAGIC?	29
VULNERABLE ENOUGH TO LOSE CONTROL	43
A MESSY MIDDLE	57
WHY YOU ARE NOT SAYING YES	70
WHEN YOU SAY NO TO YOUR INTUITION	94
WHEN YOU SAY YES TO YOUR INTUITION	104
WHY WE SUFFER	114
SCIENCE MEETS INTUITION	123
GETTING UNSTUCK & ACCESSING FLOW	142
YOUR NEXT INTUITIVE STEP	161
INTUITIVE INVITATIONS	171
THE FREEDOM OF AN INTUITIVELY LED LIFE	182
GOING DEEP	191
A PROMISE TO YOURSELF	206
ACKNOWLEDGEMENTS	213
ABOUT THE AUTHOR	215
PRAISE FOR AUTHOR	216

Copyright © 2023 Jennifer Jane Young Say Yes to your YES
ISBN: 978-1-7382509-0-5

No part of this publication may be reproduced, stored in a retrieval system, or transmitted in any form or by any means, electronic, mechanical, photocopying, recording or otherwise, without the prior written permission from both the copyright owner and publisher.

Disclaimer All the information, techniques, skills, and concepts contained within this publication are of the nature of general comment only and are not in any way recommended as individual advice.

The intent is to offer a variety of information to provide a wider range of choices now and in the future, recognizing that we all have widely diverse circumstances and viewpoints.

Should any reader choose to make use of the information contained herein, this is their decision and the authors and publishers do not assume any responsibilities whatsoever under any condition or circumstances.

For more information about the publisher, Jennifer Jane Young, or for additional trainings, speaking engagements, or media inquiries, please visit: www.jenniferjaneyoung.com, or contact:
info@jenniferjaneyoung.com.

Book design by: Guillaume Séguin

DEDICATION

I dedicate this book to my two beautiful nephews, Victor and Noah. May this book give you the courage to trust your gut and never settle for anything less than what you dream of. Every courageous step I have taken since you were born has been for you, to show you that anything you feel in your heart and gut is possible. Je vous aime mes amours.

I dedicate this book to my mom, who has supported every single crazy leap I have taken in my life, even when it terrified her. Mom, your support has allowed my dreams to come true. I could not have made it to forty years old having lived such an expansive life without you. Thank you for being by my side, supporting my journey, and picking up the pieces when things were hard.

To my younger self. I knew my truth all along and should have never doubted myself. I was never broken.

To every beautiful soul who has an inner yearning for the life they truly want. Just say yes, and your intuition will lead the way!

MAY THIS BOOK
LEAD YOU TO
YOUR SOUL'S
DEEPEST DESIRES.

INTRODUCTION

Do you ever fear waking up in five, ten, or twenty years disappointed by all the things you didn't do because you were terrified to fail? Maybe you didn't take action because you didn't know where to start. Or you ignored things out of worry for what other people would think of you.

Let me introduce myself. My name is Jenn, and I'm an expert at taking risks. After spending my teenage years lost, confused, and suffering from feeling like I didn't fit in anywhere in this world, I decided that the pain of staying where I was was worse than the fear of taking leaps into the unknown and failing. This became a guiding principle in my life. Any time it has felt painful to stay where I am, I know it's because I was stopping myself from saying yes to something my intuition was guiding me towards or something I needed. I was living in limitation because of fear.

Entrepreneurship was the life raft that saved me from a limited life that was causing me debilitating anxiety and deep discontentment. Until I started taking these intuitive leaps, there was no flow in my life. I kept hitting the same walls, struggling with the same problems, and landing in the same frustrating place. In high school, for example, I was often kicked out of class for disruptive behavior because I couldn't sit still or focus. I often ended up in the principal's office or what they used to call "The Hole," a small room with no windows that you would have to spend the entire day in and were not allowed to leave until school was out. All the "bad" kids were sent there, the ones I now like to call the creatives or entrepreneurial ones. When I have tried to fit into a box, conform to what society was telling me to do, or bypass my gut, I have experienced friction in my life. High school was just the beginning of it.

I eventually came to realize that the most successful entrepreneurs are intuitive leaders. I've read so many stories of how Richard Branson, Oprah, and Sara Blakely (to name a few) have built their incredible successes by trusting their gut and making decisions from that place of inner wisdom, even if it didn't make any rational sense.

Entrepreneurship, when I discovered it, became kind of like my home. It also helped me come home to myself. It allowed me to relax into who I was in my most natural state and find my flow, which I like to define as our path of least resistance. I began to recognize that when I followed what my intuition was telling me to do, I would experience ease and flow instead of friction and frustration. Without this realization, I could have easily settled for a life that felt too small for the big visions and feelings I had inside. (So many people do!)

But one day, when once again the pain of staying where I was felt bigger than the fear of taking a leap, I decided to begin following my intuitive nudges and say yes to a dream I had been holding inside of me for years. I wanted to become a yoga teacher. So, I got out of my head and made it work.

I took my summer vacation, found a one-month, intensive yoga teacher training, and dove right in. That moment was pivotal because it was the first time I truly said yes to a strong, intuitive nudge. That was the moment that launched me into entrepreneurship. It was scary, I had no plan, no money to support this crazy leap, and I had no idea how to be an entrepreneur. All I knew was that I wanted to experience more than what my life was then, and I craved the freedom that came with following my flow.

From the moment I booked that teacher training, nothing was the same anymore. From the moment we say yes, the universe starts its work and life begins to adapt for us.

When I went to work after that training and tried to fit myself back into the box that was my old life, I was faced with constant friction and conflict. The pieces didn't fit anymore because I had expanded, and my life had expanded as well. My experience now was all too big for the experience I was trying to squeeze myself back into. You can step out of the limitations of your current situation as well because there is a life raft waiting for you. Just say the "Y" word and the universe will immediately support you on your new journey.

There are days now when I wake up and wonder: "What would my life look like today if I had not taken my intuitive leaps?" Thinking of all the things I would have missed out on over the last two decades terrifies me! I might still be living a small-town life in Canada instead of living the mixed Caribbean dream life I have now, one that I had long since yearned for. I might still be in the twelve-plus-year relationship that was suffocating me and keeping me small and scared instead of experiencing three beautiful love stories that moved me through the most important healing of my life. My dog Johnny would be living and suffering in the streets of Mexico instead of bathing in love each day in our family. I would be stuck in a "job" that made me miserable, living a limited life instead of being a successful entrepreneur, publishing a book, living freely, feeling fulfilled, and making an impact in the world. So much greatness would not exist if I had not said yes to my YES. This is why I want you to learn, as of right now, why it is so important to listen to these cues and how you can find the courage to say yes to what really matters to you.

What I want you to say yes to is the everyday guidance that your intuition is sending you. Your YES is the next step, action, decision, experience that is best for you. One thing you will learn in this book is that what is best for you ends up being what is best for everyone around you—even if you think the opposite.

Your YES is everything and anything that feels exciting, intriguing, or expansive, even if it doesn't make sense to anyone else (or your logical mind). Your YES is your curiosity toward things in life that you would like to explore or learn more about. Your YES is everything that has already been aligned for you to take action on while here on this earth.

You can't miss out on life because life just happens every day with or without your participation. It moves, and we move with it. But you can miss out on living it in a way that feels good to you, settling for what you think you "should" do or acting in a way that is driven by fear. So how do you know what is a truly aligned, intuitive YES and what is not? This book will show you the way to that clarity.

Have you ever wondered why we feel so incredible anytime we go to the ocean? The ocean has always represented intuition for me. It holds all of life in it, literally. It is filled with wisdom that leads us to clarity without any words, and it always teaches us about flow. When we sit by the ocean, we feel calm, peaceful, and anchored. For some reason, we can let go more than usual. From that energy of letting go, we then get the answer we have been seeking or the idea we have been looking for. We also discover a part of ourselves we have been hiding and hesitating to express. That calm, fluid energy we feel when we go to the ocean is mirroring back that calm, fluid space that exists within ourselves, the one filled with all the wisdom we need. When we sit by the ocean, we feel connected or reconnected. When we sit quietly with ourselves, we experience the same thing. You don't need to go to the ocean to find the wisdom, clarity, answers, and the next steps you have been seeking because the wisdom of the ocean is right inside of you. It's called your intuition.

The roadmap to the life you're so deeply yearning for is inside of you, and your intuition is the compass leading you toward it. When you say yes to your intuitive nudges (your YES), you experience things you have been dreaming of, and you expand. When you ignore these nudges or say no to them, you contract and stay stuck, too small for all that truly wants to be expressed through you and for you.

Here is what I learned in that first experience of honoring my intuition. Life adapts for the brave. When you say yes to your YES, the universe adjusts to support you. Any time I have said no to my YES, I have suffered and stayed stuck. Every time I have said yes to my YES, I have expanded into more success, abundance, and happiness.

You and I are a very rare breed. We have big dreams beyond what is expected of us by our friends, family, and society. We know more is available to us, and we want to access it. We don't want to settle for what everyone else is doing. And we especially want the freedom to follow our YES—our creativity, our curiosity, our hearts! The desire to do it and the actual actions we take are what make a difference in whether we experience our dreams or not. I want this book to inspire you to listen and take action. To say yes and do the thing. If you are reading this book, you have an entrepreneurial spirit. It doesn't mean you have an actual business, but it does mean that you want the freedom to craft your life how you desire.

I want this book to elevate your personal leadership. To strengthen your courage to pursue your intuitive desires. To help you trust in the wisdom of what your intuition is telling you and trust in how supported you always are. You don't need to have everything figured out now to say yes. The path will unfold with every step forward you take. You are safe to walk into unknown territory or onto a path that is not yet fully paved. You don't need to have all the answers in order to follow your gut. Needing that confirmation or assurance is what is stopping you from saying yes. All you need to do right now is take the next step forward. I believe the yearnings you have are a preview of what is available to you if you just dare to step toward it.

Take a moment to pause here and breathe

into what you are feeling. When was the last time you really took a full breath? Your intuition is hiding right under that next breath. It speaks to us through our bodies, and it's when we slow down that we can actually feel and hear it. Many of us resist slowing down for this exact reason—but we don't know it. We are terrified to feel. We are terrified of the answers we will discover when we get quiet. Deep down, there is an invitation for everything we feel, and the unknown of that invitation can be scary and uncomfortable.

What is your intuition saying right now, even after just one breath? And what is it saying after three breaths? Is there a nudge you want to say yes to right now that could move you into expansion, more peace, ease, or joy? Maybe it's even something as simple as what you would like to eat or drink next. I have had so many friends call me on my bullshit and show me exactly what actions I have been resisting. I am so grateful for every time someone helped me see my truth when I was too scared to. I hope that this book will be the friend that will help you see yours.

When your intuition is guiding you toward something, you do not in any way need to throw your life up in the air. I mean, you might. Kind of like I did when I left a twelve-year relationship and moved to Mexico. But it's not a requirement. This journey doesn't have to be terrifying and life-altering. It can be beautiful and gentle. You get to choose. This is your life—your Masterpiece. Do with it what you want. What's most important to know is that there are no mistakes. Life is a journey of learning and growth. We spend so much time trying to find our purpose in life when really it is so simple. This is it.

To learn, grow, and discover deeper and more truthful expressions of who we are. Let's dive deeper together and see what we can discover in the depths of your beautiful soul.

But first, let me introduce myself a little more so we can get to know each other before I lead you down this path of self-discovery. We will be embarking on a transformational journey together, so I want you to know and trust me.

I don't want you to read my bio as "Jenn is some sort of guru and has accomplished all these things or has all the answers" because the truth is that I don't have the answers for you. They are inside of you, not me. I want you to read my bio as a testament to the power of intuition, both where it has led me and the experiences it has allowed me to have. Your intuition can do the same for you.

I am an Intuitive Business and Leadership Advisor and founder of The School of Intuitive Leadership. The kind of school I wish I would have had access to throughout my life and entrepreneurial journey. You will soon read about how much I suffered growing up and how broken and lost I felt. I spent most of my teenage years having nightmares about ending up as a total failure and never finding my place in the world. The School is what is missing for us rare breeds who want to live outside of the box and beyond the limitations that are placed on us. It's a place for us to learn the language of our intuition and take bold actions together toward what is meant for us.

At The School, we bridge the gap between intuition and practicality so we can take action on where our inner compass is leading us and implement our visions instead of just sitting with these beautiful dreams. I have been an entrepreneur since 2010 and have gone from yoga therapist to being a United Nations consultant, leading and mentoring a community of more than five thousand global business owners, in partnership with the International Trade Centre in Geneva, Switzerland. And today, I am a published author. You will see in my story how I was divinely guided to each of those things by my intuition and how often I resisted saying yes to these opportunities. When I was offered the position as a United Nations Consultant, I wanted to decline it, but my intuition nudged me not to. In the moment, it logically didn't fit the path I wanted to take. I am so thankful today that I didn't decline because it was transformational and eye-opening in so many ways.

As you read this book, I want you to learn how to quickly identify your own intuition and find the courage that is already inside of you to take practical steps so that you don't give up on the intuitive invitations—I promise they will never give up on you!

Are you ready to follow the compass of your intuition? If so, let's begin!

INTUITIVE REFLECTIONS

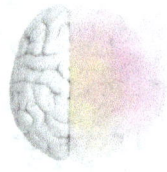

What is one thing your intuition has been nudging you towards that you have been ignoring?

INTUITIVE
REFLECTIONS

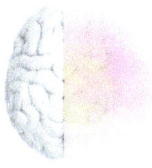

How do you feel when you think of saying yes to
that intuitive invitation?

INTUITIVE REFLECTIONS

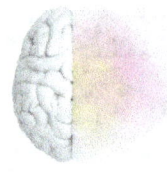

What is the worst thing that could happen and the best thing that could happen if you said yes?

> "TRUST YOUR GUT BEFORE YOU ARE READY."
>
> *– Jennifer Jane Young*

CHAPTER 1
DO YOU BELIEVE IN MAGIC?

If you don't already believe in magic, I hope that you will come to as you move through this book because that is what your intuition is—Pure Friggin' Magic. It lives inside of you each and every day, and it is really important for you to believe in this inner magic so you can access it. It's magic because it makes things happen that you could never have imagined possible. Your intuition will surprise you over and over again if you give it a chance to lead you forward. Sometimes it will tell you what to eat, sometimes it will tell you what your next leap is, and sometimes it will tell you when to say yes or no. This magic contains all the answers you could ever dream of. You know that saying "If you had a magic wand, what would you ask for?" Your intuition is like that magic wand in many ways. It contains the path toward what you desire most, the answers you are dying to receive, and the direction toward the most exciting and expansive experiences of your life.

For me, it represents something wonderful that isn't planned and that you can't quite explain logically. As you'll learn later in the book, this can be accessed in a specific part of our brain where logic is not available.

I want to start by sharing one of the most magical and unexpected moments in my life, back when my intuition had been asking me to slow down for a very long time. When I finally listened to it, it made something completely inexplicable happen. To this day, I still can't rationally explain it, but I know there was an important message for me about what is possible when we actually listen to our gut! Especially in moments of complete despair.

It was at the beginning of my entrepreneurial career when I was a yoga teacher. I was teaching the last class of my day, and I was utterly exhausted. The students in that class were like family to me, and usually, any time I went to teach them yoga, I was overjoyed. But that day, I was at the end of my rope. I had been trying to thrive and survive in this yoga career, pushing things forward and teaching about two to three classes per day. I had been teaching yoga for about two years at that point, having abandoned my career, and I was trying to survive financially. Working harder just seemed like the right thing to do. Most days, I would wake up and feel resentful of what was ahead of me. The thought kept crossing my mind: "Why is this path so hard when my intuition clearly guided me to it?"

I was running on empty in every sense. The fatigue I felt that day was so heavy that I felt like my soul was exhausted and telling me, "You just can't anymore. You need to stop." But I wanted to succeed so badly in this career and slowing down felt like failing. I didn't want to lose all the momentum I had created. Every day, I felt like I was trying to force the manifestation of my dreams and goals. I was in survival mode. When your body and mind are exhausted and at the point of exhausting your soul, then things are really not looking good. Our souls rarely get discouraged. But that day, mine was!

I arrived a little before the class, went into the yoga room, closed the door, and got into a legs-up-the-wall pose (one of my favorite restorative yoga postures to reenergize me). But this time, just getting into the pose took everything out of me. I remember settling in and wanting to cry from exhaustion. But I held in the tears so I wouldn't break down right before class. Everything about my life at that moment felt so friggin' hard.

All I could think about was finding a way to get out of teaching that class. To escape and be released of all my obligations. When we are not listening to our intuition and doing what our bodies are telling us to do, that is what happens—our whole life begins to feel like an obligation. At that point in my career, I felt like I wanted to run away from my life, take a break, and start over.

I remember feeling like I couldn't quit because there was something waiting on the other side of this struggle, yet at the same time thinking, "I can't keep going like this." I thought at that time that my success was all and only up to me, which I have come to learn is not at all the truth about how life works.

"Life is a balance of never giving up and always letting go," as I once heard from Mylène Bergeron, a yoga teacher I know.

At that moment I needed to embody that wisdom, but I didn't know what the solution was. I needed to survive financially, and I couldn't imagine myself doing anything else. I knew I was on my path, but I was suffering. The duality was confusing.

As I settled into my pose, I put my phone next to me to set an alarm, so my students wouldn't walk in on me snoring in case I fell asleep. I saw that my phone was at the end of its battery and about to die. This drop in my glass of water was just too much. I remember thinking, "F*ck it. I let go. If I fall asleep, then so be it. My students can wake me up." I didn't have the energy to take myself out of the yoga posture and go plug it in.

I closed my eyes and fell into one of the deepest meditative states I've ever been in. I remember feeling like I was out of my body, in another realm. I began to feel the reward of listening to what my intuition was telling me which was to slow down and rest. As I was resting in the posture, I was fully conscious yet not even close to being awake. There was a sense of peace in me that I had never felt before. As if a healing was happening. That feeling of letting go was both comforting and scary. My brain was trying to grip, and my heart was letting go. I began to realize how little I had rested in my life. Having gone through a lot of trauma at a young age, I had learned to live in survival mode and fight by doing more and working harder. I was a grown ass woman and had never really felt this sense of peace and relaxation before. It felt so unfamiliar and delicious. I wanted more of that. A journey of deep healing began for me that day.

My whole body started to feel lighter as if I had more space inside to breathe. Every breath felt like one of relief. I can't remember how long this lasted because it was truly an out-of-body experience. When I awoke, I felt disoriented and as if I had restored all the energy I had exhausted in my life by overdoing myself because I wanted so badly to succeed.

I remember thinking, "How am I going to teach in this state?" I was calm and grounded, but it was as if I could not fully come back yet to my physical, human reality. I dragged myself out of the posture and was immediately snapped out of my foggy state by what I found.

I took my phone in my hands to look at the time, and I found the battery completely charged! My phone battery was at 100 percent. I stared at my phone for about ten minutes in total confusion. I was trying to logically figure out what happened back there when I was in that state. As my body and soul recharged when I finally let go, so had my phone. What the fork?

I've often heard that spirits on the other side use electronic devices to communicate with us because it gives them an easy channel to access us in this physical realm. This is when I began to understand that this whole journey I was on and what I was trying to create was definitely not all up to me. Something out there, something that I could not physically see, was helping me as I took each step forward in my life. I like to believe that when we get an intuitive nudge, it's our guides speaking to us through our physical bodies and trying to tell us to listen so they can jump in and help us. Help is what came to me that day in my yoga posture. This is the kind of magic that happens when we listen to our intuition!

INTUITIVE REFLECTIONS

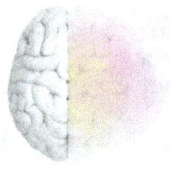

Can you recall a magical moment in your life that happened when you released control a little bit?

INTUITIVE REFLECTIONS

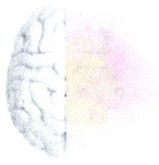

On a scale of 1-10, how full is your cup right now (1 being empty, 10 overflowing)?

INTUITIVE REFLECTIONS

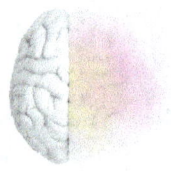

What is your intuition telling you that you need right now to be more aligned, healthy, and vibrant so you can live a better life?

> "INTUITION IS INTELLIGENCE."
>
> – *Jennifer Jane Young*

CHAPTER 2
VULNERABLE ENOUGH TO LOSE CONTROL

In 2016, when traveling to Mexico, I fell in love and decided to leave my twelve-year relationship, leap out of my safe and comfortable life in Canada, and move my ass and my dog to Cancun, Mexico. It was one of the biggest fights of my life between my intuition and my ego. Other people's judgments and fears were coming at me like the speed of lightning, and my own fears and judgments were stepping in to make me feel like I was a complete nutball to even think about doing this. But I was stuck, miserable and so badly craving a different life—one I knew I couldn't access from where I was at that moment.

It took so much courage and vulnerability to say yes to that invitation from my intuition. I had to move past my biggest fears and step into the most unknown I had ever experienced. New country, new language, new friends, no family. Just me and my dog, Bailey. We figured it out and stepped into one of the most expansive journeys of our lives. Now, sitting in Mexico in a Caribbean-style house that was once on my vision board, living a life that matches my soul's desires, I can see why I was being invited to take that huge leap of faith in 2016.

It is 100 percent impossible to live and lead an intuitive life without being vulnerable and willing to let things get messy, willing to make mistakes, and willing to step into the unknown. Living intuitively inevitably means taking risks, and when we take risks, we move through a temporary discomfort that can feel like failure.

In order to take risks, we need to be vulnerable because on the other side of risk is the unknown, a scary place to go sometimes. Being vulnerable is an act of courage. It is probably one of the bravest things you can do. Each time you trust your gut and take a risk to follow that invitation, you are being brave.

It can be easy to feel like following our intuition is reckless. We can feel insecure and worried about failing if we try to follow something that we don't know will work out. But that is the beauty and magic in living intuitively. When we act from our right brain where creativity, intuition, and imagination live, we are giving ourselves the opportunity to experience infinite possibilities. In that infinite space, anything is possible. Some experiences are enjoyable and some less so, but in that space, we will always live more fully with fewer regrets.

If you only follow your left brain—where all that is accessible is what you already know and what you have already experienced—and choose to live safely, you will keep experiencing the same thing over and over again in different forms. This is why we often get bored and restless in our lives and work. We are not allowing ourselves to live on the edge of growth and transformation, to try something new and temporarily be mediocre, to do something just for the pleasure of it and not care about results, or to take a leap of faith and be vulnerable and willing to be in the mess while we discover a treasure.

How boring would life be if we had all the answers? We get to play in life with our intuition, using it to help guide us to our next answers, steps, actions, and decisions, just like solving a treasure hunt. Do you remember those when we were kids? They were so much fun! I believe that we can still have fun as adults, discovering the daily treasure hunt that is our lives. We don't need all the answers. We just need to step into the unknown and explore.

There is a simple way for you to know if you are taking an intuitive risk or a reckless risk: observe your energy. If it is calm, excited, curious, and you feel expansion in your body, that is your intuition. If you feel urgency, tension, pressure, and contraction in your body, that is recklessness. All our answers lie in our beautiful bodies, through which our intuition speaks to us. If you just slow down, breathe, and practice deep listening, you can find so many answers and solutions. Your intuition can sense what you can't yet see, and it will always tell you or show you through sensations.

We live our lives doing the same things over and over and over again. Therefore, we spend most of our lives in our left brains, in what we know. Approximately 90 percent of our thoughts are the same thoughts as the day before and approximately 70 percent of these thoughts are negative ones.[1] In order to break that obsessive thought-loop you need to break your habitual way of going through your day. Although I believe in having healthy rituals, things you can lean into during your day that nurture you in a positive way, I also believe that it is really important to change things up and do something different so you can have a different experience and open yourself to a new perspective. Something as simple as having your morning coffee in a different place can crack open your creativity. When you do something different, unusual, or unfamiliar, you are allowing new parts of your brain to open up. This changes everything up to the actual cells in your body.

It allows you to experience a new and different version of yourself, unlocking potential you didn't realize you had, seeing a solution that was in your blind spot, or landing on a creative idea that could drastically shift things in your life. Your comfort zone is a good place to rest, and we all need to be there sometimes. We need moments to pause and integrate (like while reflecting on the questions at the end of each chapter). If we were constantly growing, we would exhaust ourselves. But if you want to live a truly fulfilling life, you need to regularly live outside your comfort zone.

One of my favorite mentors, Richard Branson, encourages people to prepare for the worst-case scenario. He is one of the most inspirational intuitive leaders I have known. His whole life has been led and lived intuitively, and because of that, he has created and experienced incredible things. You are so much stronger, resourceful, and capable than you could ever imagine. When you are thinking of taking an intuitive leap, I encourage you to journal on two things:

What is the worst thing that could happen?

What is the best thing that could happen?

Both are possible, and you are capable of handling it all!

We will never understand the why before we take the leap. If we did, we wouldn't benefit from the transformation that comes with these kinds of decisions and actions because we would then micromanage every known detail. We wouldn't open our hearts, stretch our minds, and let our souls explore in the same way. We would live the experience from our heads because we would already know the plan and purpose of our action.

What's important when you take these kinds of leaps (big or small) is to take really good care of yourself and your nervous system along the way. What do you need to feel safe and supported to follow your YES and do the thing? Don't answer this from your head, answer it from your heart.

Maybe you need to shut out other people's opinions or meditate every morning to ground yourself. Maybe you need to journal to release any stress from your nervous system or hire a coach or therapist. Put in place the things you need to have the courage and vulnerability to say yes to your intuition and start stepping into the experiences you want to live. Be your own guru, lead yourself forward in the most loving and supportive way, and you will be capable of saying yes to anything you desire—even when it's scary!

INTUITIVE
REFLECTIONS

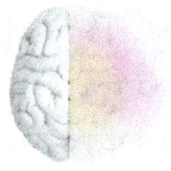

What meaning do you give to making mistakes or not getting things right?

INTUITIVE
REFLECTIONS

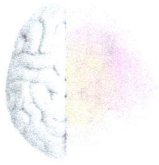

How do you feel when thinking about being vulnerable and taking imperfect action?

INTUITIVE REFLECTIONS

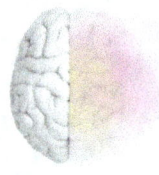

What is one imperfect step forward you can take right now towards an intuitive invitation that you are feeling?

> "IT'S ALWAYS AND ONLY ABOUT THAT ONE NEXT STEP."
>
> – Jennifer Jane Young

CHAPTER 3
A MESSY MIDDLE

You might not want to trust me after reading this story, and you might even question the validity of what I've written. If you don't believe me, there are no hard feelings—I promise. This is what our left brain does. It tries to deny any kind of information that it can't explain logically, which is why so many of us live our lives in safety and comfort instead of taking leaps on our gut feeling. The truth is that I don't really want you to trust me. I want you to trust yourself. I want you to finish reading this book feeling like you just learned a new language—the language of your intuition—and having the courage to take imperfect action in the direction it is guiding you. What I am sharing with you in this book is my truth: my raw honest experiences of following my own gut, the lessons I have learned, and the magic that has happened for me. Your story is going to look completely different.

I have never regretted following my YES, and even when things got messy after doing so, I understood that it was happening to help me expand into the next phase of my life—the one that would allow me to grow more and experience life at a deeper level. This path is not always one of safety and comfort initially. It can be messy and confusing because our brain makes us feel anxious and worried about doing things outside of the pretty, paved path it has planned for us. This journey is less of a yellow brick road and more of a rustic path where you need to whip branches out of your face as you walk through the woods. But you always end up in a big, beautiful opening like at the end of the movie Little Foot.

There will be moments of transition, times in between taking action and landing in the new place, when you might feel like you've made a mistake or you can't handle what is coming for you. But what I can say from my experience is that those fears are just monsters under the bed. They mostly exist in our heads, and they are there to ensure that we are not being reckless. There is nothing wrong with fear. It has many messages for us, like showing us that we are stepping out of our comfort zone and growing, or like reminding us to look both ways before crossing the street so we don't get hit by a bus. You just need to learn to use it in the right moments and leverage it for your own growth and success.

As I write this book, I am in the midst of the messy middle that comes after saying yes to our intuition. It is important for me to share these stories with you because I want you to know that living intuitively "theoretically" doesn't work. You need to actively answer the call of your inner compass to truly live an intuitive life and get the subsequent rewards.

When I followed my gut in 2016 and moved to Mexico, I realized it had been a quiet whisper speaking to me since I was a teenager. I never understood why until I traveled there. All those whispers were confirmed, and I knew in my gut that a part of my journey was meant to take place there.

My journey there was exciting, expansive, scary, and also challenging, but it was something I needed to go through in order to be who and where I am today.

There were people and situations waiting for me in Mexico that helped me grow in ways I could not have in my safe life in Canada. They helped me heal things by facing challenging experiences that pushed me way out of my comfort zone. When I initially arrived in Mexico to start my new life, I was so insecure and full of internal emotional pain. The experiences I went through while living there for four years brought up my deepest wounds, biggest fears, and most paralyzing insecurities—and I was invited to face them all. I had the biggest breakdown of my life followed by the biggest breakthrough of healing and growth. My intuition led me to exactly the right place to experience what was necessary for me to live fully and shed everything that was keeping me small and suffering.

When COVID hit, my gut told me I needed to go back to Canada. After four years of growing, healing, and stretching myself out of my comfort zone in Mexico, it was time to come back to my roots and rebuild a new foundation from there. We can't always be taking intuitive leaps. We need moments to pause between expansive moments in our life. We need to be still, assimilate, and rest. I was moving into an incubator of rest and renewal that was desperately needed. It was time to cocoon and process the last four years. The caterpillar-to-butterfly process is a perfect example of the natural cycles of life we must go through and the beautiful dance of expansion and contraction that is necessary. Every step has a purpose, and if we allow ourselves enough time to slow down and get quiet, our intuition will tell us when it's time for the next phase. As I am writing this chapter right now, I am sitting in a café, waiting to go to an interview to get my Mexican residency again. Yes, I am on my way back to Mexico on a new journey. Why? I have no idea. All I know is that when I went back to visit Mexico a few months ago, after being away for two years in my cocooning phase, a little voice inside was very clear in telling me that I needed to go back. Since I said yes to that intuitive nudge, I have gone through all the feelings. Although our intuition is clear and calm, the journey after we say yes can be a mix of many things. This messy middle is often when people give up because they think they have made a mistake. We have this idea that when we follow our gut, everything should be smooth sailing. But that is so very inaccurate. Sometimes it is easy, but most often, while life is adapting for you, things will feel messy and unstable. Don't let that transition moment make you doubt yourself in any way.

The reason I share this is not to scare you but to help you get ready to experience an exhilarating ride after you have answered your gut and to remind you that you have everything inside to take this journey. You are stretching yourself beyond your comfort zone and into new, unknown territory, and that will come with some discomfort. There is a quote from Hunter S. Thompson that I love that speaks perfectly to the difference between living a safe, comfortable, guaranteed life versus an imperfect, expansive, daring one. "Life should not be a journey to the grave with the intention of arriving safely in a pretty and well preserved body, but rather to skid in broadside in a cloud of smoke, thoroughly used up, totally worn out, and loudly proclaiming "Wow! What a Ride!"[2] In the last few weeks after saying yes to moving back to Mexico, I have celebrated, experienced incredible excitement, cried, grieved for leaving my family again, faced anxiety, had thoughts that I was losing it, and reconnected with a sense of curiosity I have not felt in a long time. Embrace it all, and most importantly, don't fear the unknown of what comes after you say yes. Let yourself feel; you are safe! That is the gift of life. It's like opening a Christmas present every morning. If you knew everything you were going to experience in advance, there would be no excitement or mystery for what is to come. Imagine how flat life would be if we lived it without any wonder. There would be no space for dreaming, imagination, and creative thinking. The unknown is the gift. Relish the mystery!

INTUITIVE
REFLECTIONS

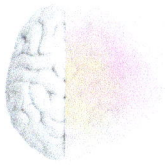

What are you curious about that you could start exploring just for fun?

INTUITIVE
REFLECTIONS

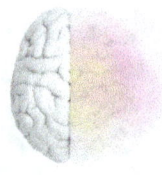

Where could you let your life get a little bit messy so that you could try something new?

INTUITIVE
REFLECTIONS

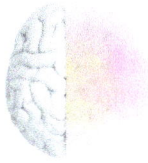

What is one routine you could change up in the
next week to flex a habit of yours?

> "LIFE NEEDS YOU WHERE YOU ARE AT YOUR BEST."
>
> – Jennifer Jane Young

CHAPTER 4
WHY YOU ARE NOT SAYING YES

Intuition is part of your DNA. If you are a human being who lives and breathes on this planet, then you are intuitive, so you can check that box of "I need to become intuitive" and simply relax into that, knowing that now all you need to do is learn to hear and trust it. We don't doubt that animals have instincts, right? Intuition is the human version of instinct in animals. It's a guidance system that is built into us to help us make decisions in our lives. We also have an animal instinct that protects us and takes care of our survival. So, we essentially have a double guidance system. Our intuition will nudge us on everything from small things, like what our body needs for breakfast, to bigger things, like when it's time to hire someone in your business or leave a relationship. The answers are always right inside of you. Strangely we often look outside ourselves to make decisions.

If we get real and honest with ourselves, we know what we want to say yes to, but fear gets in the way of following our intuition. When we have fearful thoughts—which are created by the left-brain sending messages to the sympathetic nervous system to try to protect us—we go into fight or flight mode. We imagine all the things that could go wrong and begin experiencing those scary thoughts as physical symptoms in our bodies simply from thinking about them.

Our mind tries to prove to us that our YES is not logical and way too risky. Then, we stay stuck, and we let our YES slip between our fingers.

Here are the most common issues I see that get in the way of extraordinary humans like you leading their lives intuitively and why many of us end up leading with our heads instead.

Problem #1: Your intuition is speaking to you, but you can't hear it.

We live in a fast-paced, noisy world, and by letting ourselves be guided by the outside world, we create a lot of static in our internal system. Like driving through fog, it's really hard to know where you are going or where you need to turn next if you can't see clearly in front of you. The noise of the outside world is like fog. Hearing your intuition is really difficult when your energy is always outward-facing instead of turned inward.

The reason: You are in your stress response.

When the sympathetic part of our nervous system is dominating, our internal rhythm is moving fast (breath, blood, lymph) which then activates the left side of our brain (rational thinking, control, fear, worry, etc.). In that state, we shut down our intuitive channel, our creativity, and our problem-solving skills. If you imagine being chased by a bear in the middle of the woods, you will get an idea of how you might feel in your body and how your mind will respond. In this state, you can do crazy things, like maybe jumping off a cliff to get away from the bear instead of calmly seeing a solution that could save your life. This is when we can actually be reckless.

The solution: You need to slow down.

With my background in yoga therapy, I can't help but bring the understanding of the nervous system into my teachings because it brings all of the pieces together to help us understand how our incredible body, mind, and soul work together. In our day-to-day lives, we often make decisions from a place of urgency, stress, and overwhelm. We end up depleted and without experiencing the results we desire. Enter anxiety and a life of obligation! Slowing down and doing less so that you can feel what is happening in your body is what will allow you to hear the wisdom of your intuition. When you allow yourself to feel, you actually regulate your nervous system.[3]

I once found myself stuck in the fog of a very abusive relationship. For four years, my intuition was trying to send me information, but I couldn't hear it. I was high on love drugs, trying to rationalize and fix everything from my head (left brain). I kept trying to do more, be more, do better, be better. I was obsessively overdoing and overcompensating out of fear. It felt safer to try to fix the situation than to get quiet and hear the truth.

This is one of the main reasons why we miss the cues from our inner wisdom: we are scared to feel the truth. And when we slow down, that is exactly what happens. So, we numb ourselves with overdoing, staying busy to avoid the information we need to live a better life. This landed me in a nervous breakdown, caused me to lose my health, and led me onto a long journey of deep healing. I don't regret any of it because I finally brought myself to a place where I could see the damage my trauma was causing. This experience was transformational. It woke up my intuition and made it stronger than it has ever been before in my life.

Now, I get to use what I learned in this experience to help others listen to their intuition faster, so they don't have to go as far as I did and end up in a breakdown. But if you do go as far as I did, it's completely okay, too. There is no perfect way to live intuitively. It is not a linear experience. You learn through the mess and become a stronger, wiser version of yourself along the way. It's also part of the healing journey. If you stay small and safe, you miss out on opportunities to heal past trauma that is keeping you stuck! My stories are there to serve as a mirror for you and encourage you to be brave and bold in your life.

Problem #2: We hear our intuition, but we don't trust the information we are

receiving.

Our intuition sends us information that we sometimes don't want to hear or that doesn't make any kind of logical sense to the left brain. Our brain and nervous system are always seeking known or safe information. When it's logical or familiar, it feels safe, and when it's not, we often just ignore intuitive information coming our way—sometimes intentionally and sometimes without even realizing it.

The reason: The intuitive information we are receiving doesn't seem practical or convenient, so we hesitate to trust it and act on it.

This is where most people get stuck! If the information you receive gets immediately categorized by your brain in the unsafe zone because it's unfamiliar or not logical, you will most often not take action. You will go into analysis paralysis, overthinking, trying to find common sense to give you permission to say yes and follow your gut. In this space, people can wait years and even a lifetime before saying yes to their YES. Many people never do at all!

The solution: Don't try to rationalize your intuition.

Our brain and ego interrupt the intuitive flow of information to tell us that it is not safe to follow that nudge because their job is to keep us safe. It sees that YES as the bear chasing us through the woods. We need to remind ourselves that there is no danger and give ourselves permission to continue exploring the intuitive information that comes through, just one step at a time. We need to nurture a calm internal environment so that when we receive information from our intuition, we can welcome it feeling calm, confident, and curious instead of scared, worried, and doubtful.

Here's the great thing about intuition, it will keep speaking to you even if you put the information aside for a bit. You don't need to worry about losing that nudge that came through. You can sit with your insight while you help your brain understand that it is safe to listen to it. There should never be a sense of urgency to listen to your gut. The most powerful thing you can do is to start taking small actions in the direction of your intuition because you will see the wonderful things that happen when you do. In turn, that proof will help your brain and nervous system release control and relax into the experience.

When I visited Mexico for the first time after leaving and felt that strong intuitive nudge inside telling me I had to come back, I kept thinking, "What is even happening?" Just two years before, I had sold everything I had in Mexico, put my dogs on a plane, and flew back to Canada to start over again. To top it off, my intuition told me that the way back to Mexico this time was by car, driving six thousand kilometers (twenty-seven hundred miles) across three countries. I was finally healing from my nervous breakdown and was worried this would be too much for me. Plus, I was just starting to settle into a new life in Canada.

What I did know for sure though is that I was feeling uninspired living in Canada. Lifeless almost, like a plant I forgot to water for too long. Even though it didn't seem logical to make this trip back to Mexico, it felt like a YES in my entire body. The intuitive guidance was so clear!

When I landed back in Cancun for the first time after leaving, I felt vibrant, alive, and inspired. That was the confirmation that told me I had made the most aligned decision for myself. I had taken it a few steps at a time, listening to what my intuition was telling me I had to do next until I made it back to Mexico. Sometimes, we need to take a first step forward to confirm if it is intuition or not. Whether you take a giant step or a baby one, it doesn't matter because you can always course correct along the way.

My first step before making it back for good looked like this: Three months after that trip when I felt like I needed to move back permanently, I took a flight back to Cancun and stayed for one month to work from there and be in the day-to-day life again. Not by the beach or drinking mojitos. In an apartment, with my laptop—working. I needed to know if what I was feeling was a need to close a chapter, if my ego was being attracted to something bright and shiny (like how the grass is always greener somewhere else), or if going back to Mexico was truly in alignment for me. Turns out it was in alignment. So, I kept taking next steps until I moved back permanently.

There was a process I needed to go through to find my clarity. It was scary, overwhelming at times, and very questionable. It was not logical or rational, but it was aligned for me. If you keep looking for logic, waiting for confirmation that everything is going to work out, or wanting to keep things neat and tidy, you are never going to experience what you truly desire and what you came here for.

Problem #3: We hear it, we trust it, but we don't know how to get started and take the next step.

We say YES, we are ready to take the leap and then....BLANK. We are frozen and don't know how to take action on this big, beautiful insight we just had. Our overanalyzing and need to think of the perfect step forward stop us from taking one imperfect step forward into the unknown. This one imperfect step is what will give us the clarity we are searching for to embark on this intuitive journey.

The reason: You are looking at the whole path instead of just that one next step ahead of you.

One of my favorite quotes is from the Yiddish expression "Der Mensch Tracht, Un Gott Lacht," meaning "Man plans, and God laughs." Planning and overthinking are ways of procrastinating on our intuition. If you are looking for a guarantee before trusting your gut, you probably won't find it, and this is when we stay stuck and settle for what is instead of saying yes to what could be.

The solution: It's always and only about the one next step forward.

Once again, our brain kicks in and starts micromanaging this magical information that just came through. Our brains are beautiful. They are what allow us to function in this human experience, what keep us safe and keep order in the world. You just need to know when it's time to be in the left-brain mode (logical, structured) and when it's time to be in the right-brain mode (creative, fluid). It's always and only about the one next step forward. Our brains try to plan out the next two hundred steps, which is why we get stuck. The whole plan becomes overwhelming, and then we lose the high vibration and clarity we had from our intuitive insight.

The solution here is to go deeper within yourself, get quiet, and simply ask, "What is one small, next step in the direction of this insight?" Look for the breadcrumbs leading you forward. There is no point in trying to plan everything out because things will most likely change along the way. But that one next step will open the door to the next and the next and the next. All you need to do is consistently get quiet with yourself to hear where your intuition is guiding you and follow that compass.

When I came out of school, certified and ready to be an early childhood educator, I thought I had everything all figured out— finally! I had finished a program (for once in my life) and had stability and a consistent paycheck. I was thriving and so good at my job. The kids loved me, the parents loved me, and everything seemed perfect (like we were told it should be). But resentment quickly kicked in, and I found myself once again wanting to get the f*ck out. There was no space for my whole self, my creativity, my spontaneity, or my leadership. Everything that wanted to be expressed in me was being stuffed back down in a safe, little box just so I could live a good and stable life.

Yoga came into my life when I was a struggling teenager full of rage, anxiety, and rebellious energy. A friend of my mom's recommended yoga and abstract painting to help ease my intensity and transform that energy into creativity. This was one of my most life-changing moments because arts and yoga became a vehicle that allowed me to express myself fully, process my emotions, and channel my creativity.

Every time I would go to a yoga class, I

would look at the teacher and feel this pull in my tummy. "This is what I want," I would hear. "This is the kind of role model I want to be in my life. This is the kind of impact I want to make."

When we start feeling these intuitive nudges, we really need to pay attention because life sends us hints and breadcrumbs to confirm our intuitive information through sensations in our body. We often call this a full-body YES!

Interestingly, the daycare where I was working decided to integrate yoga for the kids, and my curiosity and passion started to grow even more. These were breadcrumbs being dropped onto my path. I had no idea what to do with this incredible feeling inside of me, so I just kept listening to it to see what else it wanted to tell me. I almost did nothing with it. But through the yoga teacher who came to the daycare, I discovered a yoga teacher training that was being given during the summer. I booked my summer vacation and went to that training. That was my one little step forward. It was the only thing I felt clear in doing so I could explore this further.

After my summer vacation, I came back to work for a few weeks as a changed person. It was impossible to fit back into that tiny box. Not long after, I quit my job and threw myself into what I now know is entrepreneurship. There were a million baby steps after that—one after the other. Accumulated, they have made me who I am today: an Intuitive Business & Leadership Advisor & former United Nations consultant now living my dream life with my dogs in Mexico.

Don't stay stuck in analysis paralysis. Just

take one step, then another toward the life that is waiting for you. And every time you hesitate, think about what is waiting for you that you are missing out on. Let things get a wee bit messy so you can create a masterpiece with your life!

INTUITIVE
REFLECTIONS

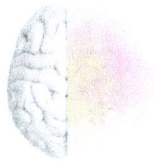

What is one step you can take towards a yearning
you have been feeling for a while?

INTUITIVE REFLECTIONS

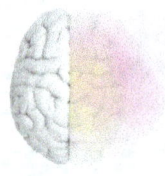

How would it feel to let things get a little messy for the sake of a more expansive experience of life?

INTUITIVE
REFLECTIONS

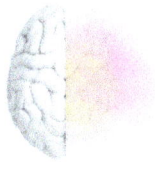

How will you feel in 3-5 years if you continue to ignore your intuitive nudges?

"LOGIC WILL BRING YOU TO THE SAME PLACES YOU HAVE ALREADY BEEN."

—Jennifer Jane Young

CHAPTER 5
WHEN YOU SAY NO TO YOUR INTUITION

Growth happens on the other side of our comfort zone. Becoming the leader we came here to be requires us to leap beyond what we know, safely bypass logic, and take calculated risks. Only by doing this can we truly live the life that is calling us inside and have all the success, abundance, joy, love, creativity, impact, and unimaginable growth that we are truly yearning for.

When we don't listen and trust our gut, we

settle for safety and comfort. We continue dreaming of the life we want instead of really living it, and we miss the opportunity to have the life that is actually calling us. THAT life, the one you can feel inside of you, is the one that will allow you to fulfill your purpose, make your mark, experience a deep flow state in your work, and enjoy rich experiences in your personal life.

We feel exhausted and discouraged because we aren't getting the results we have been working so hard to create. It seems like no matter how much we do, we are not experiencing what we truly crave because our actions are not aligned with our intuitive knowing.

We get stuck and feel frustrated from being trapped in a vicious cycle that lands us in the same place, over and over again. Welcome to the Groundhog Day of your life! We wake up feeling the unexpressed potential inside of us. We feel like results and abundance arrive in tiny droplets. We are not making the impact we know we are capable of. We struggle financially because we keep settling for just enough instead of the infinite potential available to us. We fall into the victim spiral and drain our energy by complaining about our lack of results, success, and joy. Fun times! Can you relate?

There has been a theme in my life of saying no in moments when my intuition was asking me to say yes to its guidance. That theme has manifested as staying in relationships past their expiry date and sacrificing my happiness because I was too scared to listen to my gut and get out when it was time. This happens to me in intimate relationships, work relationships, and friendships. Maybe you will recognize one of your themes through my stories.

Because of my past experiences as a child, I learned to be the peacekeeper. I then grew into an adult who silenced herself and her needs in order to keep all the pieces together, not cause anyone harm, and not suffer myself by avoiding conflict. Life will offer us the same kind of experiences repeatedly until we heal the thing inside of us that is causing us to make harmful decisions. In the moment, it feels like punishment, but it's actually an act of love from the universe. It's a gift in disguise. It's an offering from your guides, giving you another opportunity to release that pain inside so you can live more freely and joyfully.

Over the years, I've stayed in an abusive relationship too long with a narcissist and ended up in a nervous breakdown. I've stayed in a friendship too long that was disempowering me and causing me to completely disregard my values and truth. I've stayed in work relationships too long that took advantage of my generosity, landing me in burnout. No one did this to me, I chose it. I was frustrated from landing in the same place over and over again, yet I kept making the same decisions that brought me suffering until I had the biggest breakdown of my life. That breakdown, which I now call a breakthrough, brought me to my knees and to the depth of my soul—of my truth. It allowed me to see why I wasn't saying yes to the wisdom of my intuition.

The experience brought me face to face with my inner wounds that were crying for attention, and I was finally able to sit with myself and look at my truths, my needs, my pain, and my deeply hidden desires. All of those things I just mentioned, the ones we are so scared to look at, really aren't that scary. When we do finally acknowledge them and give them some space to speak to us, we access a path leading us to deep healing which allows us to then access our true desires, and we can finally fulfill them, which then helps us stop making harmful decisions.

Remember, the actions you are not willing to take or the decisions you are not willing to make are the ones that will change your life.

INTUITIVE
REFLECTIONS

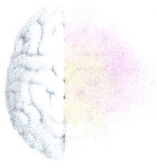

What have you recently said no to that you know deep down was a yes?

INTUITIVE REFLECTIONS

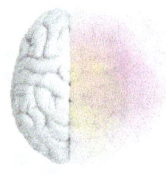

What do you need to heal inside of you to create space for more joyful, free, and inspired living?

INTUITIVE
REFLECTIONS

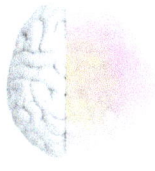

What is the pattern that you are stuck in that you continue to experience over and over again?

> "IT'S WHEN WE ARE HAVING FUN THAT WE DISCOVER WHO WE REALLY ARE."
>
> – *Jennifer Jane Young*

CHAPTER 6
WHEN YOU SAY YES TO YOUR INTUITION

When you say yes to your YES, you unlock the flow of everything that is trying to enter your life and you graciously accept the gifts that the universe has been trying to give you. The floodgates begin to open! You are saying yes to the big, beautiful impact you came here to make. You are saying yes to becoming the best version possible of yourself. You are saying yes to living an incredible life, instead of an okay one. You stop settling and you start living fully. You stop having to work so hard to experience what you yearn for. Instead, you take intentional actions that create exponential results.

Your manifestation process transforms, and you begin to seamlessly embody the 80/20 rule.[4] Instead of putting in 80 percent of effort and experiencing 20 percent of results, you are only putting in 20 percent of aligned action and experiencing 80 percent of the results you are actually yearning for. Not just any results, the ones that you truly want and that are good for you.

Let me share an example of how I am now doing work that is aligned, easeful, and successful. As you now know, I'm an Intuitive Business & Leadership Advisor. It took me a really long time to own the intuitive piece of my work. I used to call myself only a business advisor. I tried to "left brain" my title constantly because I had a lot of fear concerning adding the word "intuitive" before my title. I had this idea that adding that word would discredit me somehow in the world of business and leadership, even though I have over a decade of experience supporting startups to six or seven-figure businesses and successful leaders. That wasn't enough for my small left brain to trust in taking this leap. But my intuitive side kept creeping into all my work. No matter how much I tried to stuff it away and hide it, it kept clawing its way back. My intuitive nature was weaving its way into all of my work—and my clients were loving it.

Your intuition will never give up on you!

It will whisper. That will feel like a little nudge. If you don't listen, it will speak louder. That will feel like being tripped while you are walking. If you still don't trust it, it will shout. That will feel like being stopped in your tracks. Finally, if you still have not acted on its beautiful wisdom, it will scream. That will feel like being lovingly slammed to the ground.

This happens not to punish us but to show us that the path it is guiding us toward will be so much easier, nourishing, and abundant than the one we are on now.

Before saying yes to owning the word "intuition" in my work, I was struggling. My work didn't feel fluid. I felt like I was wearing the wrong pair of shoes, and my work was surface level. When I finally took the leap and added the word "Intuitive" to my title, no surprise, I started to feel so much more momentum pick up in my business. I was a United Nations consultant, even while calling myself an Intuitive Business and Leadership Advisor. People started to get curious about how intuition can become part of business-building. They started to tell me, "Yes, this is what I have been needing" or "This has been the missing piece for me" or "This is how I want to lead my life and business." I really believe that the intuitive nudges (the YESes) we are resisting are the exact things we need to be doing. I used to teach this in my yoga classes all the time, reminding my students that the pose they hated the most was the one they actually needed.

This is where the creation of my signature quote and guiding principle came from: "The actions you are not willing to take or the decisions you are not willing to make are the ones that will change your life." I recently lost a team member in a company I am leading, and before leaving, he told me that my previous quote is what inspired him to take the leap into a new, expansive career.

I was sad to lose him and also so incredibly proud that he was taking a leap and saying yes to his YES!

Every time I trust my gut, something new expands in my life. Each time, it's like opening a gift on Christmas morning. Who here doesn't want to open a gift?

Leading our lives intuitively is all about focusing on what matters most to us. This is not a one-and-done deal. It's a daily practice that you must cultivate to build confidence as you witness the positive effects ripple each time you say yes to your intuition.

INTUITIVE
REFLECTIONS

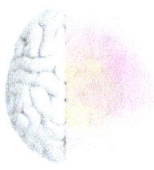

If you let your imagination tell you a story, how would it paint your life of YES?

INTUITIVE
REFLECTIONS

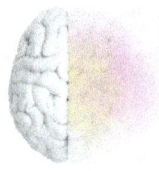

What is something new and unknown that you would love to experience?

INTUITIVE
REFLECTIONS

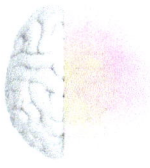

Remember a time that you did listen to your gut.
How did that roll out? How did you feel?

> "THE FREEDOM YOU ARE SEEKING IS ON THE OTHER SIDE OF FEAR."
>
> – Jennifer Jane Young

CHAPTER 7
WHY WE SUFFER

The pain of staying where you are when you know it's no longer right is much worse than the temporary fear that comes with saying yes.

It became very clear to me that the moments in which I was suffering throughout my life were when I was not listening to that inner voice trying to guide me toward what was most aligned for me. Saying no does not always entail actually saying, "no."

Simply ignoring or not answering the call of your intuition is a way of saying no as well. So, when I would say no—directly or indirectly—I would block the flow of what was trying to come into my life, which is always what is good or better for us.

It's painful to live a life that is out of alignment, to not let ourselves receive the full potential of what is available to us and trying to come into our lives, or to not take action because we are scared.

It's like trying to walk with shoes that are too small for our feet, or a plant needing to grow but being stuck in a pot that is too small. Do you feel like your pot is too small for your big, beautiful soul and potential? Transplant the damn plant so it has more space to grow! For us to be able to grow, expand, and receive more, we need to give ourselves bigger pots, and that comes from trusting and taking action on our gut. It requires getting comfortable with taking risks, letting go of what no longer serves us, and letting life get a little messy.

Our intuition knows where we need to go to grow. We stop ourselves from saying yes because our left brain (logical, rational) is trying to keep us in that safe, small pot. To be fair, that is its job. But our left brain doesn't understand the universal laws of life. If you leave a plant in a pot that is too small for too long, it will begin to rot and die. It can't breathe. It has no more space to be. This is how we feel when we don't step forward toward where our intuition is trying to guide us. We end up feeling frustrated, small, stuck, and like we are slowly dying inside. We often feel frustrated that we are working so hard and we are not receiving the opportunities, money, success, or love that we actually desire. But it is actually right there, fighting to come into our lives. It's wanting to flood in, but we are blocking it by not following the guidance of our intuition.

Who signed up for that? Not me! And if you are reading this book, my sense is that you didn't either. Let's explore what else is possible for you if you give yourself permission to take up more space and follow the guidance of your inner wisdom. To do that, you need to learn how to master your nervous system. So, let's talk about this beautiful internal system that you have that is in charge of either making you feel expansive and relaxed or stressed and contracted.

Don't stop here! I know it's tempting to drop the book as soon as you hear me talking to you about the brain and the nervous system. Learning about the incredibly wise suit that you live in each day, your physical human body that carries you around, is one of the most empowering things you can do for yourself. And I promise, I will make this a fun and inspiring learning process!

INTUITIVE
REFLECTIONS

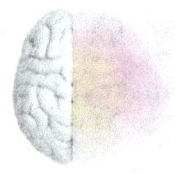

What metaphorical shoes feel too small for you right now? (e.g., work, marriage, home, community, daily routine, etc.)

INTUITIVE
REFLECTIONS

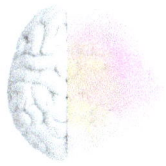

Where do you feel like you are suffering in your life right now?

INTUITIVE REFLECTIONS

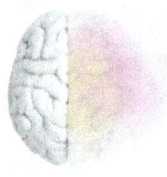

Who could you become if you gave yourself a bigger pot to grow in?

"RELEASING YOUR CONTROL IS WHAT WILL FREE YOU TO LIVE HOW YOU TRULY DESIRE."

— Jennifer Jane Young

CHAPTER 8
SCIENCE MEETS INTUITION

Both our intuition and our ego want us to feel safe but in very different ways, and you will understand the difference once you understand how your nervous system works. Trying to figure out if something is intuitive or ego-driven guidance is probably one of the biggest struggles people have when it comes to leading their lives intuitively. How can we know if what we are feeling is truly intuition? The truth is that it's not always easy to define intuition versus ego. I believe that the solution to this is to practice. We get clarity when we take action and when we slow down. Again, there is no perfect way to do this. Sometimes, we figure things out by moving into action, and other times, from stepping back and doing nothing. You need to move past the fear of making a mistake and just try. It is the only way you will be able to get to know and master taking intuitively driven action. That said, I won't leave you hanging in this vague space. I have some practical tips on how you can begin defining intuition (right-brain guidance) from ego (left-brain motivation).

First, I would encourage you to ask yourself if you have felt this urge before. Is it something that started as a whisper and has been getting louder and louder, as we spoke about earlier? Remember, your intuition won't abandon you. If there is a sudden sense of urgency, such as "If I don't do XYZ

I will fail, die, or my life will fall apart," chances are that is not intuition. If you feel like you are going to "lose" something and you can sense attachment, that is probably your ego. It wants to keep things under control, so any sign of micromanaging and trying to hold things together is not intuitive wisdom. Intuitive guidance could be hiding under that left-brain conversation, but action taken from that place will be led by your ego instead of your wisdom. Since we know that intuition will never give up on us, we can trust that it will come back to speak to us if we haven't acted on it. We will be shown over and over again what we are being invited to do, so there is no need for urgency. Take a breath.

Intuition will feel more like a wise friend coming in to remind you of what is truly best for you. Like the friend who gently tries to help you see that you are in a bad relationship. You know they are right, but it feels scary to end it. The feeling that this relationship is not good for us will keep coming back, even if our brain tries to "fix" it. What is best for us will keep knocking at our door. From there, it is up to us to take intuitively guided action.

The beauty is that the action doesn't need to be perfect. The universe doesn't care if we did it perfectly or kept our shit together. The only thing that matters is that you listened and did your best to move forward. You can always take a next action to clean things up later, but when you say yes to your inner wisdom and go with it, you unlock flow to move forward.

Another question you can ask yourself is, "Does this feel like an obligation?" Intuition feels light, fun, exciting, and scary (but a good kind of scary, like when you are on a roller coaster about to fly down that peak hill). It's scary AF and exhilarating! Anything that has ever felt like an obligation in my experience has not been aligned with what is best for me.

I would also encourage you to remove expectations of how the results should look. When we try to control the what and the how, we are coming from our logistical left brain. Instead, tap into your fluid, creative right brain where possibilities are limitless! My training and career in Yogatherapy has allowed me to develop a way to help my clients understand how they can thrive versus struggling and surviving.

There are also two types of fear we tend to experience. Left-brain fear and right-brain fear. Left-brain fear is coming from our sympathetic nervous system and all the memories from our past and our conditioning. This brain chemistry is secreting cortisol (stress hormone) in your body, trying to keep you safe from danger. Sometimes the danger is real but most often it is not. It is often fear of something irrational or very improbable, like the monster we used to think lived under the bed. Right-brain fear is more like an exhilaration. Right-brain chemistry is secreting dopamine (happy hormone) in your body, telling you that something scary and really exciting is about to happen, like the feeling you would get before jumping out of a plane to go skydiving or before your book gets published in front of thousands of people. It's a sensation of stretching yourself beyond your comfort zone into something new, unknown, and exciting. Because we all have nervous systems, there will always be a little bit of cortisol because our body will always work to keep us safe. But when it's an intuitive YES, there is more dopamine than cortisol. Knowing this will help you start to define the difference between an ego-driven or an intuitive-driven YES. Here are two examples.

Ego-driven (left brain) fear: If I don't post three times per day, every day on social media, my business will crash and burn.

Intuitive-driven (right brain) fear: If I take this business opportunity that feels exciting, I will feel uncomfortable for a while as I level up my skills AND this could bring my career and life to a whole new level.

At The School of Intuitive Leadership, we help our members stay in the right-brain lane!

Our left brain takes care of logic, analysis, structure, organization. We need our beautiful left brain, but we don't want it leading the way when it comes to growth, transformation, evolution, and creativity. The left brain makes sure we stay safe, small, and comfortable. It often makes us believe that those big, beautiful leaps we want to take, the exciting things we want to create, or the decisions we want to make that feel so damn good in our body are dangerous! When our left brain takes the driver's seat, it stops us from making intuitive decisions that will allow us to grow, reach new levels of success, create bigger impact, and experience the expansion and transformation we have been yearning for.

Would you let your dog drive your car?

Have you ever let your dog tag along for a car ride, gone in quickly to the store (when it's not hot, obviously), only to come back out and see your dog sitting in the driver's seat? If you don't have a dog, I'm sure you have often seen one do this.

That is exactly what our left brain does as soon as we are not paying attention. It takes the driver's seat even though it is not qualified to lead the way towards an expansive life. So, would you let your dog drive the car? Probably not (or at least I hope not). You don't want your left brain to drive either if you are trying to move out of your comfort zone and towards expansion!

The formula is simple. Let your intuition and creativity, which live in the right brain, move you forward and lead the way, and use your beautiful left brain to help you figure out how to make things happen in a way that is not reckless. When we do this, we experience flow.

Although the formula is simple, actually doing it is hard because it requires us to reprogram our nervous system, to think and be in a brand-new way, hence changing some deep-rooted habits we have been functioning with for most of our lives. We have, unfortunately, been taught to lead with our left brain, so we all need to untangle this conditioning in some way.

When you are feeling like your life is too small or you keep getting stuck, you are not broken, you're just human. Your formula for making things happen is just backward, causing things to be much harder than they need to be. Now, let's connect the dots between the nervous system, our brain, and our intuition to bring this all together.

Our nervous system has two parts to it. There's the parasympathetic nervous system and the sympathetic nervous system. Our sympathetic nervous system is our stress response. It is the part of our nervous system that allows us to run for our lives if a bear is chasing us in the woods. Today, the bear looks like "I'm going to die if I don't do 20,000 social media posts this week for my business," as I already noted in the example. Our nervous system reacts the same way with today's fears, as with past fears and dangers like being chased by a predator when we were living like cavemen and women. This is why we often wake up with the 3 a.m. scaries, worrying about things that feel like a life-threatening danger but aren't actually.

In the life we are living today, our sympathetic nervous system is, unfortunately, more active than our parasympathetic nervous system, which is our rest/digest or relaxation response. Our intuition is available to us when we are in our relaxation response. It is not as easily available to us when we are in our stress response. The more that we do things to activate our parasympathetic nervous system or relaxation response, the more we train our nervous system to not feel like it needs to be running away from a bear every single moment of our lives.

It feels scary to stop hustling because we feel like everything is going to fall apart and our survival is going to be at stake. We think we are not as valuable if we are not doing more but the "more" is a trap because it's never enough. It's actually the complete opposite. It's when we start to slow down, it's when we start to get quiet that we hear that crystal-clear wisdom coming through, which is intuition. And then we get that one next step that we need to take. And that next step is the one that creates the positive ripple effects that then create the life we want to be living.

What I teach is how to place the right brain (intuition, creativity) into the pilot's seat, and the left brain (logic, analysis) in the co-pilot's seat so you find the path of least resistance and access your highest level of potential, success, impact, and fulfillment. You can use my guided meditation on activating the right brain in the book resource portal available to you at sayyestoyouryes.com/resources.

In the right brain, we can access unlimited potential. In the left brain, we access limited potential. In the left brain, we can only access what we know, what we have already experienced, our conditioning, and proven data. It is a comfortable, safe, and stable space to work and live in, but it is not expansive. Growth just doesn't happen in the left brain. It happens outside of our comfort zone and in brand-new creative territory!

When you lead with the right brain and let your left brain assist you in bringing potential into form, you tap into new creativity, find solutions and paths forward, create incredible pieces of work, access higher levels of success, experience ease and flow, and so much more. We need our beautiful left brain because it is what helps us make things happen and bring things into form. We just don't need it leading the way for creative expression and expansion.

If you lead from the left brain—which is limited and structured—and then try to squeeze your right brain's big, beautiful creativity and intuition into the small left-brain box, you are killing the potential available to you, and you end up creating and experiencing the same old results, only inching your way forward toward success. It looks like a whole lot of effort for breadcrumb results instead of fluid, easy action that offers expansive results!

Put simply, think about what happens if you place a glass on top of a candle. The flame would go out because it lacks air. That is what happens to your inner flame when you put it into the small container of your left brain.

INTUITIVE
REFLECTIONS

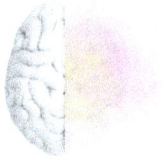

On a scale of 1-10 how relaxed do you think your nervous system is (10 being the most relaxed)?

INTUITIVE REFLECTIONS

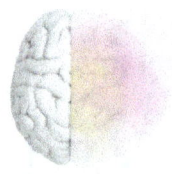

In which ways do you think your left brain constantly tries to keep you small and safe? What past experiences or traumas have kept you stuck in fear?

INTUITIVE
REFLECTIONS

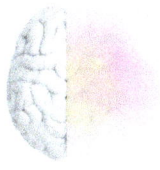

What is one way you could play in the right brain
lane today in your life or in your work?

> "YOUR SIMPLE PRESENCE HAS ENOUGH VALUE TO CHANGE THE WORLD."
>
> —Jennifer Jane Young

CHAPTER 9
GETTING UNSTUCK & ACCESSING FLOW

We. All. Get. Stuck! It's a human thing, so please don't beat yourself up when this happens. There is wisdom in stagnation and procrastination. An opportunity to pause and listen deeply to what wants to happen next. When I get stuck, I always ask myself, my guides, or my tarot cards, "What do I need to know or do next that is highest and best for me and those around me?"

Throughout my yoga years, I developed a

process that helped me identify where I was stuck, why I was stuck, and what I needed to do next based on the energy I was in. This process is a highly intuitive one that requires deep listening and connecting to your body because our intuition and inner wisdom speak to us through our body, which is why you need to learn about and love your human suit.

I call this process "The Intuitive Art of Making Things Happen," and it is inspired by the Doshas in Ayurveda, which are essentially our unique constitution. You can listen to the Masterclass at sayyestoyouryes.com/resources. An article on Deepak Chopra's website says the Doshas are "the three energies that define every person's makeup. Getting to know and appreciate your dosha is key to knowing yourself. It provides clues for what you should eat and what things you should address when your energy gets out of whack."[5]

This process of getting clarity on my next step based on the energy I am stuck in has been life-changing for me. There are three Dosha types, which I like to help people understand through the characters in the NBC series Friends. They are also related to the energies of Intention, Action, and Letting Go—the three main action categories we need to step into in our day-to-day lives. We tend to have one or two Doshas that predominantly make up our constitution and how we generally move through the world. Each Dosha can be in and out of balance which causes different reactions and states of being as you will see next. After I have helped you understand each energy, I will bring it all together to show you how you can intuitively course correct to find your flow again.

Pitta (a.k.a. Monica in Friends)

Pitta is mainly related to fire and our solar plexus chakra, which is related to our personal power, confidence, and self-esteem. Pitta energy is what allows us to move forward, take action, and digest, to name a few things. When we say yes, we are tapping into our Pitta energy.

A balanced Pitta energy is when we can confidently act and make decisions from a calm place of personal power. It is when we can move forward and digest life with ease and flow.

An imbalanced Pitta is when we are taking too much action and forcing things forward. It is when we are obsessively doing the same thing over and over again from our rigid left brain, hoping for different results. We feel frustrated, angry, and can easily burn out in this state. Physical symptoms that can show up when our Pitta energy is imbalanced are heartburn, exhaustion, and physical tension in the body and mind. Pitta often becomes imbalanced at the end of summer when we are overheating. Our bodies are overflowing with sunshine and heat, and we are burnt out from all the movement of the summer season. Our bodies start to crave slowing down, big sweaters, and Hygge vibes.

Monica in Friends flows between a balanced and imbalanced Pitta. I love how they portray her imbalanced version with humor. It always reminds me to not take myself so seriously when I am abusing of my Pitta energy and just chill the f*ck out.

The imbalanced Pitta/Monica is when she is obsessively trying to get Chandler to workout, knocking at his door before sunrise in Season Two . Or when Chandler hires a cleaning lady for her, and Monica obsessively watches her every move as she cleans the house in Season Eight, trying to micromanage. Or when she cleans her big vacuum with her little hand vacuum in Season Ten. You just want to throw a bucket of cold water on her so she cools down. That is too much Pitta energy!

Vata (a.k.a. Phoebe & Joey in Friends)

Vata is mainly related to the energy of air, the third eye chakra, and crown chakra where we access our creativity, expression, desires, and intuition. Vata energy is what allows us to dream, flow, get insights, and be creative. It's when we are connected more to our right brain and playing with infinite possibilities. It's when we can relax enough to explore our creativity without needing any specific results. When we can just be. A balanced Vata energy is when we are able to go with the flow, follow our curiosity, and harness creativity when it comes without overthinking or analyzing it. It's when we can access our intuition and follow it in the most fluid way. It's when we are easygoing and relaxed about life, taking things one moment at a time.

An imbalanced Vata energy is when our fluid energy is not grounded enough which makes us flaky and inconsistent. Then, Vata energy turns into anxiety. Our intuition, creativity, and ideas are all over the place, and we don't know where to channel our energy, so we are just floating around with no purpose. We have a million ideas and are not taking action on them. Vata often becomes imbalanced at the end of autumn, in November when there are no more leaves on the trees and outside is wet, cold, and grey. We have a feeling of being anxious and uncomfortable and we begin to crave the heaviness of winter to ground us and slow us down because we are still riding the high energy of summery Pitta without any roots to hold that energy in place.

Joey and Phoebe constantly flow between balanced and imbalanced Vata energy. They are the fun, relaxed, sometimes ditsy ones who soften the energy in the room and make you forget about everything else.

When Joey and Phoebe become imbalanced, they become too flaky in their work, for example, and end up not having enough clients/gigs, thus becoming starving artists. One great scene that represents Joey out of balance in his Vata is when he injures himself in Season Six and has a hernia but doesn't want to go to the hospital because he forgot to renew his insurance. Or when Phoebe goes running in the most I-don't-give-a-f*ck way with Rachel in Season Six and embarrasses Rachel (although, I think we all need to tip a bit out of balance like that sometimes).

Kapha (a.k.a. Ross in Friends)

Kapha energy is mainly related to earth energy and the first/second chakras which are all about safety, security, family, home, self-esteem, and pleasure.

Kapha energy is what allows us to feel calm, centered, and organized in our lives. With our Kapha energy, we structure the ideas and creativity that come through in the Vata energy. It's the energy that allows us to plan our week in our calendar or KonMari our homes.

A balanced Kapha energy is when we have our shit together in the most calm and grounded way. It's a slower-moving energy, like the elephant. It's slow and steady like the workhorse. Kapha energy has a clear plan for the week and knows the direction to take in advance. It's the energy that allows us to process what we experience and digest.

An imbalanced Kapha energy becomes lazy, lethargic, and depressive at an extreme. Things become too slow, like digestion and the flow of energy. We sit with ideas, plans, and desires and do nothing with them. We sit with our unfulfilled dreams and feel guilt and shame for not acting on them. Kapha often becomes imbalanced near the end of winter when our bodies have not been moving for many months and we have been eating warm, heavy foods. We begin to crave the fresh outdoors, blooming nature, and lighter foods.

Ross also swings between balanced and imbalanced Kapha energy. Generally, he has his shit together. He has a stable job and life, has a schedule and sticks to it, and follows his solid life plan. But when he goes overboard in his Kapha, he becomes anal, whiny, and annoying.

The best scene in Friends that represents Ross when he is out of balance is the night he has his award event—"The One Where No One's Ready"—in Season Three. He is trying to micromanage everyone to be exactly on time with the schedule and because of that, no one is actually cooperating, and things just get worse. He is literally a pain in the ass. You can actually see all the characters in their best Dosha act in that particular scene.

So, what about Rachel? Rachel is actually Tri-Doshic, which means she is pretty evenly balanced between Pitta, Vata, and Kapha. She's easy going, has her shit together, and takes action on what she wants. This is probably why so many of us connect to her character in Friends. We dream of being the cool, balanced, successful woman that Rachel is. Like everyone else, she does fall out of balance sometimes, but she pretty quickly comes back to her centered, happy self.

I love this process of tuning in to see where you have more energy in this moment of your life because it is very intuitive. The only thing you really need to do is pay close attention and practice deep listening to your energy and body. You will feel when you are out of balance in one of the Dosha's because you won't feel great in your body and mind.

If you're angry, exhausted, and micromanaging, you are out of balance in Pitta and what you need is more Vata energy to cool you down, bring in more lightness, and let go a little.

- Take a day off and wander.
- Eat a fresh salad full of raw veggies.
- Sit on the floor and play with your dog.

If you're anxious, scattered, and don't know what to do next, you probably need more Kapha energy. This helps you to ground yourself and find some inner calm in your current energetic chaos so that you can then tap into your Pitta energy and take clear actions and steps forward.

- Go do some gardening and get your hands in the earth.
- Do a grounding restorative yoga practice.
- Put pen to paper and map out your thoughts, ideas, worries, and next steps.

If you're feeling tired, heavy, and are procrastinating, like Eeyore's energy in

Winnie the Pooh, you probably need some fiery Pitta to get energy moving through you again and get your blood flowing. This way, you can find that next wave to ride and get moving.

- Do something...anything to move your body.
- Eat some spicy food.
- Take a cold shower.

If you take some simple actions to balance your energy, you will be back in your intuitive flow in no time and feel much better.

The KonMari Method is actually a great example of Doshas in balance.[6] You first start by taking everything out and throwing it into one big pile (Vata). Then you intentionally sort out what you love and don't to make a keep pile and a throw pile

(Pitta). From there you sort and organize what you are keeping (Kapha).

We will never be consistently balanced. Life just doesn't work that way. It is meant to fluctuate and be an imperfect beautiful mess. But when we go way off tilt and feel crappy, it's good to have a simple intuitive practice that can bring us back to alignment. I often lean into the Japanese philosophy of Wabi Sabi to remind myself just how imperfect and impermanent life is meant to be. It reminds me that I can accept and relax more in my current experience and trust my intuition to take that next aligned step forward.

INTUITIVE
REFLECTIONS

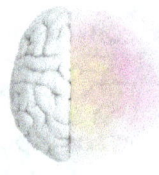

Which Dosha or character in Friends do you most relate to?

INTUITIVE
REFLECTIONS

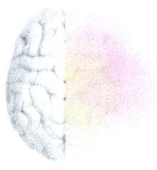

Where and how do you find yourself most often out of balance?

INTUITIVE
REFLECTIONS

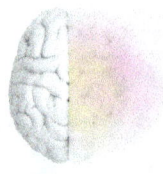

How does it feel to give yourself permission to be a beautiful, imperfect, fluctuating, messy human being?

"GETTING OFF TRACK IS PART OF STAYING ON YOUR PATH. IT'S BY GOING THE WRONG WAY THAT YOU REMEMBER THE DIRECTION YOU ARE MEANT TO TAKE."

- Jennifer Jane Young

CHAPTER 10
YOUR NEXT INTUITIVE STEP

Life is always and only about that one next step. One of the reasons so many people stay stuck in analysis paralysis is their left brain is trying to plan the next thirty-five thousand steps before taking any kind of action. The thing is, even in the next five steps things might drastically change in a way that will mess up your whole plan. Overplanning beforehand so that you are ready to take action is a waste of time and energy.

Instead of planning, I like to encourage people to envision or forecast. It leaves a lot more space and flexibility for things to change as they need to because every step and action you take is going to create a ripple effect forward which will intuitively guide you to that next place, decision, or action. Planning is more rigid, whereas forecasting or envisioning is more playful and curious. It leaves room for more possibilities than a structured plan yet still gives you some security in having a sense of direction. However, if the direction changes, you don't feel like all the work you put into your plan has been lost.

If you take a moment to tune into that beautiful gut of yours and listen to your inner wisdom, where is it guiding you right now? What is it asking of you? Before you move into the fear and overwhelm of how big this request, action, or change might feel, ask yourself, "What is one simple thing I can do today to move in that direction to just see what happens?" If you want to see how you feel, how life adapts to your actions, and what happens next, then the formula looks like this:

- Listen deeply and trust the guidance—your YES.
- Take one simple action or step in the direction of that guidance (there is no "perfect" step, so don't bother looking for it).
- Pause, observe, and see how it feels. Get comfortable with the uncomfortable and unknown you are stepping into.
- Based on your observations and how you feel, choose the next step that feels intuitively aligned.
- Repeat to keep moving in the direction of your inner wisdom that is guiding you.

- Listen to my audio lesson on listening to your intuition (before it makes sense) at sayyestoyouryes.com/resources

This is the process I walk my clients and community through. One of my past clients, let's call her Julie, experienced one of the most beautiful stories of transformation from this simple process.

She was a university professor with a very stable job and life, yet her soul was not okay with that life. She began experiencing health issues to the point of having to take a sick leave. During that sick leave, she decided to start a coaching business. When we met, she knew she couldn't go back to her old, stable life, but she was terrified to let the stability go and leap onto this new path that was calling her. The security of the money, the title, the benefits, and the retirement fund were keeping her attached to a life that wasn't fulfilling her. Her nervous system was in the stress response, as it didn't feel safe for her to make this decision.

I gently led her through a one-year process of making only one intuitive decision at a time. All these tiny steps, when accumulated over a year, allowed her to keep her nervous system in the relaxation response, unlocking her creativity, new ideas, and paths forward. Julie now has a thriving business, her body is healing, and she is living expansively instead of in the small, safe box that ended up making her sick. She could have easily settled and stuffed herself back into that tiny box and suffocated her potential for the rest of her life, but she didn't.

You don't need to either!

Can you see how much less stressful this is? You don't have to have everything figured out before you begin. There is space for play, exploration, and course correction, and you get to take little risks on what feels good and exciting. The result?

Infinite possibilities and potential.

Higher chances of experiencing what you actually desire.

More freedom and flow in your life.

Healing—oh so much healing!

It's such a good feeling and you deserve to experience this and move beyond the barriers of a rigid life that has been created from your rigid-thinking brain.

INTUITIVE REFLECTIONS

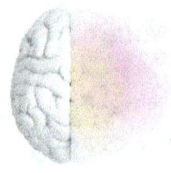

What is the box that you are currently living in that feels too small?

INTUITIVE
REFLECTIONS

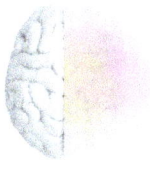

What support do you need to courageously take one step out of that box and into the unknown?

INTUITIVE
REFLECTIONS

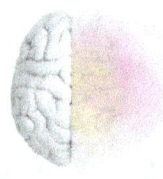

What could you achieve if you allowed yourself to feel the fear and do it anyway?

> "NOTHING IS EVER FOR LIFE. IT'S ONLY FOR NOW."
>
> – Jennifer Jane Young

CHAPTER 11
INTUITIVE INVITATIONS

When it is time for us to take the next action, make a change, or step into our next level of growth, life will always send us an invitation to that new experience. We are being invited into something all the time, but we don't always notice those invitations when they come in.

There is a concept called "confirmation bias" that partly explains why we miss these cues. Oxford Languages describes it as "the tendency to interpret new evidence as confirmation of one's existing beliefs or theories."[7] This essentially means that we look for what we expect based on what we believe.

We live with blinders on, staying focused on finding and confirming information from our past experiences and conditioning, and we miss out on all the other information and potential available to us on a daily basis. This is why slowing down and intentional/intuitive living are critical.

When we slow down enough to live intentionally, we have the capacity to go deeper inside of ourselves and actually access our truth. When we do this, there is a better chance of us bypassing our current beliefs and conditioning. We swap surface-level living for deep, intuitive living. When we are in this clear state, those limited blinders fall away, and we can see the full spectrum of life and what is available to us.

When I had just finished my Yogatherapy training, before becoming a business mentor, I was offered an invitation. Since I had become a yoga teacher, I had been taking care of my fledgling business myself. It was intuitive to me to get on my laptop and build my website, post on social media, or create marketing content. I was magnetically pulled to that every single day. But I had trained as a yoga teacher and was now a certified Yogatherapist, so my rational mind was looking for ways to grow that business. The universe pays attention to where we are being pulled intuitively and sends us invitations to continue down that path. These invitations are so precious and a key component of living a fulfilled and aligned life.

Not only was the universe paying attention to my intuitive pull but so it seemed was my Yogatherapy teacher. Throughout the training, I was always jumping in with ideas on how to grow and manage my teacher's business, but I never thought much about why I was doing this. I just did it and then kept focusing back on growing my yoga business and becoming the world's most renowned yoga teacher.

At the end of my training, my teacher Carina Raisman asked me if I would become her business manager and help her launch her new Yogatherapy School. I was both stunned and extremely excited. I felt like I had no idea how to do that, but I knew I wanted to do it. It didn't make sense with my rational plan to keep working on my yoga fame (I'm LOLing at myself right now), and a part of me felt like I was totally going off track and was about to ruin my whole career by confusing the entire world around me. But it felt like a "F*ck YES" in my body, so I jumped in.

By that time, I was starting to trust these intuitive nudges a little more. Having thrown myself out of my career as an Early Childhood Educator a few years before and leaped into yoga, I knew that life had already gotten a whole lot better since I had taken that big intuitive leap, so I figured that this time would be the same. And it is—Every. Single. Time.

Please remember this: every time you take an intuitive leap, you are building this internal muscle of trust in yourself and confirming with the universe that you want this beautiful, expansive life available to you. Then, the universe gives you more of what you desire. Just keep saying yes and you will continue to receive these life changing invitations. Some of these invitations create micro changes and others create tidal wave changes. Both are equally important.

Saying yes to this opportunity with Carina, even though it didn't make sense with the path I had planned, was one of the most important turning points in my life. Yogatherapy gave me the tools and knowledge to live in a healthy, balanced state, which gave me the pathway to access my intuition. Without this experience, I would have not learned how to access my inner wisdom so powerfully. I still use my Yogatherapy background today in my work as I teach people how to find that place of deep calm and truth by keeping their nervous system in a healthy state. But I was in love with business and helping people create their most aligned, expansive, and impactful lives through entrepreneurship. I was in love with the journey of personal growth that entrepreneurship leads us down and the power it has to help us become the fullest versions of ourselves.

Entrepreneurship has helped me see the full potential available in me and the life I am being invited into each and every day. Yoga has helped me learn to live with a calm nervous system, no matter how much past trauma I have experienced, which has helped me step out of "confirmation bias" and see beyond my limitations.

This is available to all of us, and it is what we help you do at The School of Intuitive Leadership which you can join from your book resource page. We are constantly nurturing a calm state of mind. This way, we can step into the growth that we are ready for with ease and support so that we can say yes to those invitations and experience what we came here for!

INTUITIVE
REFLECTIONS

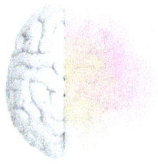

What intuitive invitations has life been sending you lately?

INTUITIVE REFLECTIONS

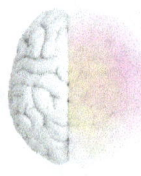

Is there something you are being called to do that feels like a YES in your body but doesn't make logical sense?

INTUITIVE REFLECTIONS

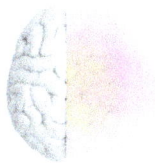

What would it take for you to take just one step forward to explore that intuitive invitation with curiosity?

> "COURAGE IS BUILT BY TAKING RISKS."
>
> — *Jennifer Jane Young*

CHAPTER 12
THE FREEDOM OF AN INTUITIVELY LED LIFE

We are all seeking this feeling of freedom, yet most of us are making decisions that lock us into more and more restrictions and contractions. Hello, life of obligation! We take a vacation, sit by the ocean, and dream of experiencing that feeling of total abandonment in our day-to-day lives. We dream of escaping our current situation and having our own Elizabeth Gilbert Eat, Pray, Love[8] experience, dropping our whole lives to go travel three countries and write our memoir. Your Eat, Pray, Love experience can start right away, where you are now because that experience is simply an accumulation of intuitive YESes. You can go to Italy, India, and Bali if you want, but you can also create your own version from this current moment. This can look different for everyone.

One way that I experience my Eat, Pray, Love life each day is by blocking off four hours every morning to do soul-nourishing things for myself. From 6 a.m. to 10 a.m., I am unavailable for anything I don't want to do or any kind of work activities. It's my time to sit with my coffee for an hour (yes, I take one hour to drink a coffee), read, spend time with my doggies, take time to make a nice breakfast, maybe go in the pool, and slowly move into my day. When I don't do this, I start my day frustrated and resentful.

This is one example of a freedom I have

because of the intuitively led life I chose. It is the accumulation of years of following YESes that created this reality for me. Saying yes to leaving my career in ECE, saying yes to the invitation from Carina to launch and manage her school, saying yes, saying yes, saying yes to all those invitations that felt good in my body even though they didn't make sense.

What is really important is not to focus on the final destination or on your big Eat, Pray, Love moment. Just keep saying yes to the small things and they will accumulate and create bigger, more sustainable experiences that will become your new reality. Nurture your nervous system every day to keep it in a calm state so that you can heal any past experiences that have created fears and beliefs that are keeping you stuck. Then, from that calm place say yes, take the leaps, and follow the breadcrumbs and invitations that are trying to lead you to your big, beautiful life every day.

You probably won't always get things right, and things will often get a bit messy. You might not always be in a calm state each time you say yes, and sometimes, you might be boiling with adrenaline before you take the leap. It's all ok. Just stay focused on what you know will help you take this path and take imperfect action so you can enjoy imperfect results, experiences, and a full life.

If you are trying to get things right, you are living from your left brain, and nothing expansive happens there. Use your beautiful left brain instead to create structure in the right places, like planning out a nurturing morning ritual that you can stick to or managing your money so you can keep having the freedom to take these leaps. Lean into the energy of your right brain and use your intuition, creativity, and imagination to say yes.

INTUITIVE REFLECTIONS

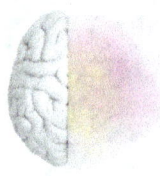

What intuitive invitations has life been sending you lately?

INTUITIVE
REFLECTIONS

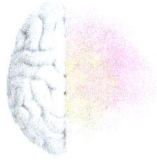

Is there something you are being called to do that feels like a YES in your body but doesn't make logical sense?

INTUITIVE REFLECTIONS

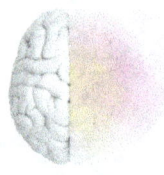

What would it take for you to take just one step forward to explore that intuitive invitation with curiosity?

"WHAT YOU ARE YEARNING FOR IS A PREVIEW OF THE POTENTIAL THAT IS AVAILABLE TO YOU."

— *Jennifer Jane Young*

CHAPTER 13
GOING DEEP

The other day, I was reading a magazine I picked up at the airport about ocean life. I love reading and learning about the ocean because it has all the wisdom and answers that we are looking for. Literally, all of life is in the ocean, and she can serve as a powerful mentor. The article was talking about life and creatures that were found in the depths of the ocean, depths that no human and most sea life could travel to. These magnificent creatures are nothing like anything we have ever known or seen. They give glimpses into possibilities that we never knew existed or could have ever imagined could exist. They are giving us information about the potential of the future.

Wisdom lies in the depths of what we don't yet know or can't see because it is not on the surface of what we know. Intuition is found in the depths of your soul. If you think about going to that level of depth in the ocean, you probably feel a sense of panic and fear set in. That is how I feel when I think of going there (if I could). I also feel a sense of excitement and wonder. And that is exactly how I feel when I dive deep inside myself, where I know my most potent wisdom, potential, and answers lie. It feels scary to go that deep because, usually, that is when we feel things that we have been covering up by living at the surface. It is where we pretend everything is all right, where we pretend we are content and settle for what currently is when our soul is screaming for more. The path to all we desire is through the channel of our intuition, which does not lie on the surface of our life.

Did you know that we were once fish? Fish, a bazillion of years ago, somehow ended up coming out of the water onto land and began developing what they needed to breathe and walk. Fish fins are what we now call our arms and hands, and fish gills are what we now call our ears.[9] If that is not mind-blowing to you, then I don't know what is. When I read that article in the magazine about how we evolved from fish, I thought, If we are wise enough to do that and have that much power to evolve, then I am totally capable of taking that next leap forward where my intuition is guiding me.

Our intuition is constantly guiding us

towards growth and evolution, and if we don't answer to it, we are interrupting important change that is meant to happen for us. That change always brings us to a better place. I know I'm quite happy being a human instead of a fish, and I'm excited about the next version of myself that I am becoming.

What you are craving is your next step forward. There is no perfect path forward, so you don't need to overthink this process by trying to find the best way ahead. Following your intuition is about living curiously and creatively. It's about trying things and taking risks. Listen to that inner nudge saying, "Hmm, I wonder how I would feel if I did XYZ" or "Let's see what kind of confirmation I can get if I try doing the thing that my intuition is telling me to do." You can't left-brain (overthink and analyze) your intuition. It doesn't work, and if you do, you will end up living in analysis paralysis, thinking about the thing or life you want to experience and staying stuck in resentment and dissatisfaction.

Be vulnerable enough to take risks and give your intuition a chance to show you what is waiting for you. You deserve this! There is a difference between risk and recklessness. If you go deep within, slow down, and practice deep listening to access the wisdom of your intuition, then you will take risks. Risks lead to growth and the chance to experience what you came here for.

Recklessness happens when we are living on the surface, half listening to our intuition and then taking impulsive, ego-driven action. This usually happens when we don't slow down enough and then our intuition (right brain) and logic (left brain) are fighting to be heard. It's as if both are yelling at you, and then you throw yourself into action from a place of urgency.

The beautiful thing is that we get wiser with practice, so if you want to feel comfortable living your life intuitively, you need to get started—here, right now, with whatever is in front of you. It's okay to feel awkward and clumsy at first. With time, you will feel more fluid in your actions.

The first time I moved to Mexico, I followed my intuition a little recklessly. I was on the verge of burnout from my past relationship and felt completely stuck in a life that was slowly killing my soul and interrupting my most aligned path, so I threw myself into a new life. But even that move, done from a place of spiritual immaturity, was aligned and exactly what I needed. I was meant to go to Mexico, but I could have taken care of my health first and done it from a different place in life that would have simply caused me less suffering.

Moving through that experience with what I knew at that time is what allowed me to step into the most important growth of my life so far. I was able to shed so much trauma and past conditioning that was keeping me stuck in a life I didn't want. So, it was messy AF, and I scared my friends and family along the way. But I survived and am now living the best chapter of my life so far.

The second time I decided to move to Mexico, I did it from a much wiser place. I knew I could trust my intuition and that I couldn't miss out on what was meant for me. The first time I went back on vacation after leaving in 2020, I got the first intuitive nudge. I had no idea how my nervous system was going to react the first time I went back to Mexico. So much happened in the first four years I was there, and I left in a nervous breakdown (now known as my nervous breakthrough). I knew I missed Mexico badly and that I felt lifeless in Canada, but that was all the information I had. As the plane was landing on my first trip back, I felt like I was preparing for a plane crash. Oxygen, check. Brace yourself, check! When the plane tilted towards the landing and my eyes gazed over the Caribbean, they filled with tears, and I began to cry. It was a feeling of being home again and coming back to what was meant for me. I could not believe the intensity of the joy I felt in my body. No fear. No trauma triggers. Nothing but pure bliss.

As I walked out of the airport, towards my friend who was waiting for me, we leaped into each other's arms and sobbed. I knew I was home and so did she. I didn't move back right away. I just trusted that calm, intuitive information and knew that I would keep taking the next steps at the right time. I went back to Canada and came back to Mexico a few months later to spend a month working, so I could be in the day-to-day life again to connect to that intuitive feeling to make sure it was still there. It was.

During that trip, I rented my new Caribbean home (the kind I had been dreaming of having since the first time I landed in Mexico). I went back to Canada with two rents to pay, ended my Canadian lease, and planned my road trip back to Mexico with my car (named "June") and my two dogs. Slowly and steadily, I came back to the life I loved, and everything aligned in the most beautiful way. Most days, I wake up in my home in Mexico, look around, and feel a wave of emotion and gratitude as I look back at the courage and vulnerability it took for me to move through all those experiences and what I get to enjoy today because of it. This is not the end. It's just a stop along the way and the more I practice living intuitively, the more I can trust in everything that happens in my life, whether those things are easy, hard, fun, or painful. As corny as it sounds, it is all happening for us!

So, here is the secret. Your left brain can't be heard in the depths. You might hear a little echo of it, but it won't be strong enough to control you or interrupt your flow. Imagine being underwater in the ocean and having someone on the beach yelling at you. You will hear their echo, but it will be hard to decipher what they are saying. When you are underwater, you hear all the internal sounds in your body like your heartbeat. It is so quiet and peaceful. Try it! Go to the ocean, or a pool, or even in your bathtub, and put your head underwater. Feel the calm and relax into the quietness. That's what is waiting for you deep inside—peace and wisdom.

"There is nothing to fear in the stillness except the awakening of your own power."[10]

INTUITIVE
REFLECTIONS

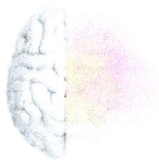

What are you scared to discover in the depths of yourself?

INTUITIVE
REFLECTIONS

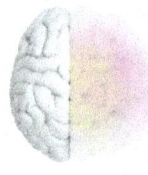

What are you excited to discover in the depths of yourself?

INTUITIVE
REFLECTIONS

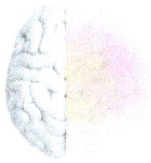

What do you need to feel safe to take that journey
into the depths of your soul?

> "YOU CAN ONLY THRIVE IF YOU ARE NOT SURVIVING."
>
> — Jennifer Jane Young

CHAPTER 14
A PROMISE TO YOURSELF

What is it that you really want? Can you say it, write it, and then own it?

I know how scary it is to do so. As I write this final chapter, I feel a lump in my throat and my eyes are watering as I remember how scary it was when I decided to move back to Mexico. I felt like I was abandoning my family all over again. I now have two beautiful nephews whom I love more than anything else in this world. They are my world. When my sister announced to my older nephew that I was leaving, his lips trembled as he said, "But we will still see her, right?" I almost canceled the whole plan that day. I felt like the worst human being in the world. How selfish could I be to disappoint my family and leave them again?

I prepped and planned for three months before hitting the road and going back to Mexico, and I cried almost every day for three months. I had to move through this grief so I could step into my next chapter. Words of wisdom from a dear friend helped me honor my intuition to go back to the life I loved. She said something along the lines of, "Jenn, you are the only one in your family truly living her life expansively with courage. Be the aunty that will inspire those little boys and who they can look up to. Be the fun aunt that they will come stay with in Mexico when they are older."

I sobbed as I heard her say those words. I knew she was right. Living my truth and offering myself what would truly make me happy was setting a positive and inspiring example for them. They would look at me and see possibilities for what they could also achieve and know that it is possible for them because they watched me doing it for myself.

Sometimes saying yes to our intuition means breaking someone's heart or destabilizing things in other people's lives temporarily. Sometimes it means thinking of yourself before someone else or making other people unhappy and uncomfortable. How other people feel about your decisions is none of your business and not your responsibility to manage. You can do things with love, kindness, and care, but after that, you don't have control over how people react. What I have learned is that everyone is allowed to have their feelings about things. It means nothing about us, and we need to give people grace and space to experience what they need. My family was really sad, and some were upset that I was leaving again. At first, I was frustrated because their feelings were making me feel guilty, but then I saw past all that and found pure love. That was all that was happening. People were loving me hard and showing me their love. When I began doing video calls with my mom after I moved back to Mexico, she said something like, "I understand now, because I can see you lit up again. You are back to the happy Jenn again, and that is what is most important."

I'm curious…How does your inner flame of joy and inspiration feel right now? Is it a tiny flame on the verge of burning out? What do you need to do to give it more oxygen so you can feel more lit up inside? Can you say yes to your gut? Be scared and do it anyway? Are you willing to experience temporary discomfort for long-term fulfillment and joy?

When I leaped out of my twelve-year relationship and safe life in Canada into a new love story in Mexico (a love story with myself) I heard that voice tell me: "The pain of staying where you are is worse than the discomfort and fear of leaping into the unknown."

Anytime I hear this voice now, I know it's time for some change.

I believe in you. You deserve the experiences that you are yearning for, and they are right there waiting for you on the other side of your fear. You can take the leap. You are more supported than you know.

To your best life!
With love, XO
Jenn

> "SAYING YES TO YOUR YES IS AN ACT OF SELF-LOVE."
>
> – Jennifer Jane Young

ACKNOWLEDGEMENTS

OMG! I wrote a book. Publishing a book is far from being a solo journey and I could not have made it to the finish line without my team of incredible humans who helped me make this happen.

Thank you...

To my editor Jeanette Smith for beautifying my words and making the experience of reading this book so enjoyable.
www.jeanettethewriter.com

To my friend and intuitive guide Maria Amore for putting the last touch of love on the words of this book before it went out into the world and for reminding me of my magic.
www.tarotwithamore.com

To my Intuitive Mentor Monica Carota for being my longtime teacher and helping me better understand the intelligence behind intuition.
www.monicacarota.com

To my book coach Alyssa Berthiaume for sitting my ass down and helping me finish this book and helping me build my book publishing team so that I could accomplish a lifelong dream of becoming an author.
www.thewriteplacerighttime.com

> "SAYING YES TO YOUR YES IS AN ACT OF SELF-LOVE."
>
> – Jennifer Jane Young

ACKNOWLEDGEMENTS

OMG! I wrote a book. Publishing a book is far from being a solo journey and I could not have made it to the finish line without my team of incredible humans who helped me make this happen.

Thank you...

To my editor Jeanette Smith for beautifying my words and making the experience of reading this book so enjoyable.
www.jeanettethewriter.com

To my friend and intuitive guide Maria Amore for putting the last touch of love on the words of this book before it went out into the world and for reminding me of my magic.
www.tarotwithamore.com

To my Intuitive Mentor Monica Carota for being my longtime teacher and helping me better understand the intelligence behind intuition.
www.monicacarota.com

To my book coach Alyssa Berthiaume for sitting my ass down and helping me finish this book and helping me build my book publishing team so that I could accomplish a lifelong dream of becoming an author.
www.thewriteplacerighttime.com

To my soul sister and creative genius Rashina Gajjar for helping me Amplify every single part of this book and book launch and never letting me see myself as less than what I truly am.
www.amplifystudio.com

To my longtime friend and incredible artist Guillaume Séguin for helping me bring the vision of my book design to life.
www.thundertoast.com

To my friend, cheerleader and international best selling author, Danielle Mendoza for generously supporting me through each step of my book launch.
www.confidentconcept.com

To my mom, for being my biggest fan, and staying by my side with each intuitive leap I have taken in my life.

To everyone who has come along my path up until my fortieth birthday, who served as my teacher, either supporting me or challenging me. I believe that every person and experience has a purpose to help you grow into your highest potential. Even those who cause us suffering. We are all just spiritual beings having a human experience, doing our best with the current knowledge we have.

ABOUT THE AUTHOR
JENNIFER JANE YOUNG

About The Author Jennifer Jane Young Jennifer Jane Young is a Canadian speaker, author, and Intuitive Leadership Advisor to entrepreneurs and business leaders around the world.

Since 2011, Jenn's leadership roles have spanned several continents, from leading a community of 5,000 entrepreneurs for the International Trade Centre as a United Nations Consultant to advising startups and multi-million-dollar businesses.

Jenn is the Founder of the School of Intuitive Leadership, a hub and online community where heart-centered, impact-driven entrepreneurs learn to embrace their intuitive wisdom, experiencing deeper transformation, alignment, and growth in their path towards success.

Through her workshops, talks, and her signature podcast, "Finding your Flow," Jenn has helped global entrepreneurs change the paradigm in how they lead their business, transforming lives in the process.

Today, Jenn is living her dream life between Mexico and the Canadian countryside, with her two rescue dogs Bailey and Johnny.

PRAISE
FOR THE AUTHOR

Praise For Author I read "Say Yes To Your Yes" in one sitting - I could not put it down! It was both engaging and informative. I learned what intuition is exactly and how I could access it. Most important for me was its positive and hopeful tone throughout: no matter how confusing and messy my life gets, I know now that courageously following the guidance of my intuition will make things better.

— Maria Amore

Praise For Author Jenn's special blend of courage, support, and creativity is something you want in your corner. Reading this book is like having her right over your shoulder helping you move towards the life of your dreams.

— Wade Bruffey

REFERENCES

[1] Christine Comaford, "Got Inner Peace? 5 Ways To Get It NOW," Forbes, April 4, 2012, https://www.forbes.com/sites/christinecomaford/2012/04/04/got-inner-peace-5-ways-to-get-it-now/?sh=5fa2cb466672.

[2] Hunter S. Thompson, The Proud Highway: Saga of a Desperate Southern Gentleman, 1955-1967 (New York City, NY: Ballantine Books, 1998).

[3] Katherine Morgan Schafler, The Perfectionist's Guide to Losing Control (New York, NY: Penguin Publishing Group, 2023).

[4] Carla Tardi, "The 80-20 Rule (aka Pareto Principle): What It Is, How It Works," Investopedia, March 7, 2023, https://www.investopedia.com/terms/1/80-20-rule.asp/.

[5] Chef Johnny Brannigan, "What Is a Dosha?" Chopra.com, September 29, 2013, https://chopra.com/articles/what-is-a-dosha/.

[6] https://konmari.com/.

[7] https://www.oxfordreference.com/display/10.1093/acref/9780199534067.001.0001/acref-9780199534067-e-1772/.

[8] Elizabeth Gilbert, Eat, Pray, Love: One Woman's Search for Everything Across Italy, India and Indonesia (New York City, NY: Riverhead Books 2007).

[9] "Secrets of the Deep," Popular Science magazine, Special Edition, January 1, 2021.

[10] Kim Krans, Animal Spirit Guidebook (San Francisco, CA: HarperOne, 2018) 133.

www.ingramcontent.com/pod-product-compliance
Lightning Source LLC
Chambersburg PA
CBHW071342080526
44587CB00017B/2924